MH00791600

# HIS AND HER'S ADVENTURES

# Travel Journal for Couples

*@ Journals & Notebooks*

*This journal belongs to*

_____

*It's wonderful to travel with somebody that you love and we never travel anywhere without one another.*

**Roger Moore**

# ADVENTURE JOURNAL

Where we started this Morning...

Where were stopping tonight...

Something I ate today...

Something I saw today...

Something I learned today...

My favorite thing about this day...

# OUT FOR AN ADVENTURE

We are going to...

First,

Next,

Then,

Finally,

We had a great time because,

We are going to...

We are travelling by...

We are  staying in...

We are going with...

# Travel Notes

Month:       Year:       Day:

Best thing there _____

_____

_____

_____

_____

Best food there _____

_____

_____

_____

_____

How much I spent _____

_____

_____

_____

_____

Something Learned about the place_____

_____

_____

_____

_____

Something to remember_____

_____

_____

_____

_____

_____

# ADVENTURE JOURNAL

Where we started this Morning...

Where were stopping tonight...

Something I ate today...

Something I saw today...

Something I learned today...

My favorite thing about this day...

# OUT FOR AN ADVENTURE

We are going to...

First,

Next,

Then,

Finally,

We had a great time because,

| We are going to... | We are travelling by... |
| --- | --- |
| | |

| We are staying in... | We are going with... |
| --- | --- |
| | |

# Travel Notes

Month:                Year:                Day:

Best thing there _____
_____
_____
_____
_____

Best food there   _____
_____
_____
_____
_____

How much I spent _____
_____
_____
_____
_____

Something Learned about the place_____
_____
_____
_____
_____

Something to remember_____
_____
_____
_____
_____
_____

# ADVENTURE JOURNAL

Where we started this Morning...

Where were stopping tonight...

Something I ate today...

Something I saw today...

Something I learned today...

My favorite thing about this day...

# OUT FOR AN ADVENTURE

We are going to...

First,

Next,

Then,

Finally,

We had a great time because,

| We are going to... | We are travelling by... |
|---|---|
| We are  staying in... | We are going with... |

# Travel Notes

Month:              Year:              Day:

Best thing there _____
_____
_____
_____
_____

Best food there _____
_____
_____
_____
_____

How much I spent _____
_____
_____
_____
_____

Something Learned about the place _____
_____
_____
_____
_____

Something to remember _____
_____
_____
_____
_____
_____

# ADVENTURE JOURNAL

Where we started this Morning...

Where were stopping tonight...

Something I ate today...

Something I saw today...

Something I learned today...

My favorite thing about this day...

# OUT FOR AN ADVENTURE

We are going to...

First,

Next,

Then,

Finally,

We had a great time because,

| We are going to... | We are travelling by... |
|---|---|
| | |

| We are  staying in... | We are going with... |
|---|---|
| | |

# Travel Notes

Month:                Year:                Day:

Best thing there _____
_____
_____
_____
_____

Best food there _____
_____
_____
_____
_____

How much I spent _____
_____
_____
_____
_____

Something Learned about the place_____
_____
_____
_____
_____

Something to remember _____
_____
_____
_____
_____
_____

# ADVENTURE JOURNAL

Where we started this Morning...

Where were stopping tonight...

Something I ate today...

Something I saw today...

Something I learned today...

My favorite thing about this day...

# OUT FOR AN ADVENTURE

We are going to...

First,

Next,

Then,

Finally,

We had a great time because,

We are going to...

We are travelling by...

We are staying in...

We are going with...

# Travel Notes

Month:                  Year:                  Day:

Best thing there _____

_____
_____
_____

Best food there _____

_____
_____
_____

How much I spent _____

_____
_____
_____

Something Learned about the place_____

_____
_____
_____

Something to remember_____

_____
_____
_____
_____

# ADVENTURE JOURNAL

Where we started this Morning...

Where were stopping tonight...

Something I ate today...

Something I saw today...

Something I learned today...

My favorite thing about this day...

# OUT FOR AN ADVENTURE

We are going to...

First,

Next,

Then,

Finally,

We had a great time because,

| We are going to... | We are travelling by... |
|---|---|
| We are staying in... | We are going with... |

# Travel Notes

Month:             Year:                   Day:

Best thing there _____

_____
_____
_____
_____

Best food there _____

_____
_____
_____
_____

How much I spent _____

_____
_____
_____
_____

Something Learned about the place_____

_____
_____
_____
_____

Something to remember_____

_____
_____
_____
_____
_____

# ADVENTURE JOURNAL

Where we started this Morning...

Where were stopping tonight...

Something I ate today...

Something I saw today...

Something I learned today...

My favorite thing about this day...

# OUT FOR AN ADVENTURE

We are going to...

First,

Next,

Then,

Finally,

We had a great time because,

| We are going to... | We are travelling by... |
|---|---|
| | |

| We are staying in... | We are going with... |
|---|---|
| | |

# Travel Notes

Month:            Year:            Day:

Best thing there _____
_____
_____
_____
_____

Best food there _____
_____
_____
_____
_____

How much I spent _____
_____
_____
_____
_____

Something Learned about the place_____
_____
_____
_____
_____

Something to remember _____
_____
_____
_____
_____
_____

# ADVENTURE JOURNAL

Where we started this Morning...

Where were stopping tonight...

Something I ate today...

Something I saw today...

Something I learned today...

My favorite thing about this day...

# OUT FOR AN ADVENTURE

We are going to...

First,

Next,

Then,

Finally,

We had a great time because,

## We are going to...

## We are travelling by...

## We are staying in...

## We are going with...

# Travel Notes

Month: _____  Year: _____  Day: _____

Best thing there _____
_____
_____
_____

Best food there _____
_____
_____
_____

How much I spent _____
_____
_____
_____

Something Learned about the place _____
_____
_____
_____

Something to remember _____
_____
_____
_____
_____

# ADVENTURE JOURNAL

Where we started this Morning...

Where were stopping tonight...

Something I ate today...

Something I saw today...

Something I learned today...

My favorite thing about this day...

# OUT FOR AN ADVENTURE

We are going to...

First,

Next,

Then,

Finally,

We had a great time because,

We are going to...

We are travelling by...

We are  staying in...

We are going with...

# Travel Notes

Month:                 Year:                 Day:

Best thing there _____

_____

_____

_____

Best food there _____

_____

_____

_____

How much I spent _____

_____

_____

_____

Something Learned about the place _____

_____

_____

_____

Something to remember _____

_____

_____

_____

_____

# ADVENTURE JOURNAL

### Where we started this Morning...

### Where were stopping tonight...

### Something I ate today...

### Something I saw today...

### Something I learned today...

### My favorite thing about this day...

# OUT FOR AN ADVENTURE

We are going to...

First,

Next,

Then,

Finally,

We had a great time because,

| We are going to... | We are travelling by... |
|---|---|
| | |

| We are  staying in... | We are going with... |
|---|---|
| | |

# Travel Notes

Month:                Year:                Day:

Best thing there _____

_____

_____

_____

_____

Best food there _____

_____

_____

_____

_____

How much I spent _____

_____

_____

_____

_____

Something Learned about the place_____

_____

_____

_____

_____

Something to remember_____

_____

_____

_____

_____

_____

# ADVENTURE JOURNAL

Where we started this Morning...

Where were stopping tonight...

Something I ate today...

Something I saw today...

Something I learned today...

My favorite thing about this day...

# OUT FOR AN ADVENTURE

We are going to...

First,

Next,

Then,

Finally,

We had a great time because,

We are going to...

We are travelling by...

We are staying in...

We are going with...

# Travel Notes

Month:            Year:            Day:

Best thing there _____

_____

_____

_____

Best food there _____

_____

_____

_____

How much I spent _____

_____

_____

_____

Something Learned about the place_____

_____

_____

_____

Something to remember_____

_____

_____

_____

_____

_____

# ADVENTURE JOURNAL

| Where we started this Morning... | Where were stopping tonight... |
|---|---|
| | |

| Something I ate today... | Something I saw today... |
|---|---|
| | |

| Something I learned today... | My favorite thing about this day... |
|---|---|
| | |

# OUT FOR AN ADVENTURE

We are going to...

First,

Next,

Then,

Finally,

We had a great time because,

| We are going to... | We are travelling by... |
|---|---|
| **We are staying in...** | **We are going with...** |

# Travel Notes

Month:                  Year:                  Day:

Best thing there _____
_____
_____
_____
_____

Best food there   _____
_____
_____
_____
_____

How much I spent _____
_____
_____
_____
_____

Something Learned about the place_____
_____
_____
_____
_____

Something to remember_____
_____
_____
_____
_____
_____

# ADVENTURE JOURNAL

| | |
|---|---|
| Where we started this Morning... | Where were stopping tonight... |
| Something I ate today... | Something I saw today... |
| Something I learned today... | My favorite thing about this day... |

# OUT FOR AN ADVENTURE

We are going to...

First,

Next,

Then,

Finally,

We had a great time because,

We are going to...

We are travelling by...

We are staying in...

We are going with...

# Travel Notes

Month:                Year:                Day:

Best thing there _____

_____

_____

_____

_____

Best food there _____

_____

_____

_____

_____

How much I spent _____

_____

_____

_____

_____

Something Learned about the place_____

_____

_____

_____

_____

Something to remember_____

_____

_____

_____

_____

_____

# ADVENTURE JOURNAL

| Where we started this Morning... | Where were stopping tonight... |
|---|---|

| Something I ate today... | Something I saw today... |
|---|---|

| Something I learned today... | My favorite thing about this day... |
|---|---|

# OUT FOR AN ADVENTURE

We are going to...

First,

Next,

Then,

Finally,

We had a great time because,

| We are going to... | We are travelling by... |
|---|---|
| We are staying in... | We are going with... |

# Travel Notes

Month:                  Year:                  Day:

Best thing there _____
_____
_____
_____

Best food there   _____
_____
_____
_____

How much I spent _____
_____
_____
_____

Something Learned about the place_____
_____
_____
_____

Something to remember_____
_____
_____
_____
_____

# ADVENTURE JOURNAL

**Where we started this Morning...**

**Where were stopping tonight...**

Something I ate today...

Something I saw today...

Something I learned today...

My favorite thing about this day...

# OUT FOR AN ADVENTURE

We are going to...

First,

Next,

Then,

Finally,

We had a great time because,

## We are going to...

## We are travelling by...

## We are staying in...

## We are going with...

# Travel Notes

Month:                    Year:                    Day:

Best thing there _____
_____
_____
_____
_____

Best food there   _____
_____
_____
_____
_____

How much I spent _____
_____
_____
_____
_____

Something Learned about the place_____
_____
_____
_____
_____

Something to remember_____
_____
_____
_____
_____
_____

# ADVENTURE JOURNAL

Where we started this Morning...

Where were stopping tonight...

Something I ate today...

Something I saw today...

Something I learned today...

My favorite thing about this day...

# OUT FOR AN ADVENTURE

We are going to...

First,

Next,

Then,

Finally,

We had a great time because,

We are going to...

We are travelling by...

We are staying in...

We are going with...

# Travel Notes

Month:                Year:                Day:

Best thing there _____
_____
_____
_____
_____

Best food there  _____
_____
_____
_____
_____

How much I spent _____
_____
_____
_____
_____

Something Learned about the place_____
_____
_____
_____
_____

Something to remember_____
_____
_____
_____
_____
_____

# ADVENTURE JOURNAL

Where we started this Morning...

Where were stopping tonight...

Something I ate today...

Something I saw today...

Something I learned today...

My favorite thing about this day...

# OUT FOR AN ADVENTURE

We are going to...

First,

Next,

Then,

Finally,

We had a great time because,

We are going to...

We are travelling by...

We are staying in...

We are going with...

# Travel Notes

Month:                    Year:                    Day:

Best thing there _____
_____
_____
_____
_____

Best food there   _____
_____
_____
_____
_____

How much I spent _____
_____
_____
_____
_____

Something Learned about the place_____
_____
_____
_____
_____

Something to remember_____
_____
_____
_____
_____
_____

"**W***herever you go, go with all your heart.*

*Confucius*

# ADVENTURE JOURNAL

| Where we started this Morning... | Where were stopping tonight... |
|---|---|
| | |

| Something I ate today... | Something I saw today... |
|---|---|
| | |

| Something I learned today... | My favorite thing about this day... |
|---|---|
| | |

# OUT FOR AN ADVENTURE

We are going to...

First,

Next,

Then,

Finally,

We had a great time because,

| We are going to... | We are travelling by... |
|---|---|
| **We are staying in...** | **We are going with...** |

# Travel Notes

Month:                    Year:                    Day:

Best thing there _____
_____
_____
_____
_____

Best food there  _____
_____
_____
_____
_____

How much I spent _____
_____
_____
_____
_____

Something Learned about the place_____
_____
_____
_____
_____

Something to remember_____
_____
_____
_____
_____
_____

# ADVENTURE JOURNAL

Where we started this Morning...

Where were stopping tonight...

Something I ate today...

Something I saw today...

Something I learned today...

My favorite thing about this day...

# OUT FOR AN ADVENTURE

We are going to...

First,

Next,

Then,

Finally,

We had a great time because,

## We are going to...

## We are travelling by...

## We are  staying in...

## We are going with...

# Travel Notes

Month: _____ Year: _____ Day: _____

Best thing there _____
_____
_____
_____
_____

Best food there _____
_____
_____
_____
_____

How much I spent _____
_____
_____
_____
_____

Something Learned about the place_____
_____
_____
_____
_____

Something to remember_____
_____
_____
_____
_____
_____

# ADVENTURE JOURNAL

Where we started this Morning...

Where were stopping tonight...

Something I ate today...

Something I saw today...

Something I learned today...

My favorite thing about this day...

# OUT FOR AN ADVENTURE

We are going to...

First,

Next,

Then,

Finally,

We had a great time because,

## We are going to...

## We are travelling by...

## We are staying in...

## We are going with...

# Travel Notes

Month:         Year:         Day:

Best thing there _____
_____
_____
_____
_____

Best food there _____
_____
_____
_____
_____

How much I spent _____
_____
_____
_____
_____

Something Learned about the place_____
_____
_____
_____
_____

Something to remember_____
_____
_____
_____
_____
_____

# ADVENTURE JOURNAL

Where we started this Morning...

Where were stopping tonight...

Something I ate today...

Something I saw today...

Something I learned today...

My favorite thing about this day...

# OUT FOR AN ADVENTURE

We are going to...

First,

Next,

Then,

Finally,

We had a great time because,

## We are going to...

## We are travelling by...

## We are staying in...

## We are going with...

# Travel Notes

Month:                    Year:                    Day:

Best thing there _____
_____
_____
_____
_____

Best food there _____
_____
_____
_____
_____

How much I spent _____
_____
_____
_____
_____

Something Learned about the place _____
_____
_____
_____
_____

Something to remember _____
_____
_____
_____
_____

# ADVENTURE JOURNAL

Where we started this Morning...

Where were stopping tonight...

Something I ate today...

Something I saw today...

Something I learned today...

My favorite thing about this day...

# OUT FOR AN ADVENTURE

We are going to...

First,

Next,

Then,

Finally,

We had a great time because,

| We are going to... | We are travelling by... |
|---|---|
| | |

| We are staying in... | We are going with... |
|---|---|
| | |

# Travel Notes

Month: _____ Year: _____ Day: _____

Best thing there _____
_____
_____
_____
_____

Best food there _____
_____
_____
_____
_____

How much I spent _____
_____
_____
_____
_____

Something Learned about the place_____
_____
_____
_____
_____

Something to remember_____
_____
_____
_____
_____
_____

# ADVENTURE JOURNAL

| Where we started this Morning... | Where were stopping tonight... |
|---|---|
| | |

| Something I ate today... | Something I saw today... |
|---|---|
| | |

| Something I learned today... | My favorite thing about this day... |
|---|---|
| | |

# OUT FOR AN ADVENTURE

We are going to...

First,

Next,

Then,

Finally,

We had a great time because,

| We are going to... | We are travelling by... |
|---|---|
| We are staying in... | We are going with... |

# Travel Notes

Month:                Year:                Day:

Best thing there _____
_____
_____
_____
_____

Best food there _____
_____
_____
_____
_____

How much I spent _____
_____
_____
_____
_____

Something Learned about the place_____
_____
_____
_____

Something to remember_____
_____
_____
_____
_____

# ADVENTURE JOURNAL

| Where we started this Morning... | Where were stopping tonight... |
|---|---|

| Something I ate today... | Something I saw today... |
|---|---|

| Something I learned today... | My favorite thing about this day... |
|---|---|

# OUT FOR AN ADVENTURE

We are going to...

First,

Next,

Then,

Finally,

We had a great time because,

| We are going to... | We are travelling by... |
|---|---|
| We are staying in... | We are going with... |

# Travel Notes

Month:                    Year:                    Day:

Best thing there _____
_____
_____
_____
_____

Best food there _____
_____
_____
_____
_____

How much I spent _____
_____
_____
_____
_____

Something Learned about the place_____
_____
_____
_____
_____

Something to remember_____
_____
_____
_____
_____
_____

# ADVENTURE JOURNAL

Where we started this Morning...

Where were stopping tonight...

Something I ate today...

Something I saw today...

Something I learned today...

My favorite thing about this day...

# OUT FOR AN ADVENTURE

We are going to...

First,

Next,

Then,

Finally,

We had a great time because,

## We are going to...

## We are travelling by...

## We are  staying in...

## We are going with...

# Travel Notes

Month:                Year:                Day:

Best thing there _____
_____
_____
_____
_____

Best food there _____
_____
_____
_____
_____

How much I spent _____
_____
_____
_____
_____

Something Learned about the place_____
_____
_____
_____
_____

Something to remember_____
_____
_____
_____
_____
_____

# ADVENTURE JOURNAL

Where we started this Morning...

Where were stopping tonight...

Something I ate today...

Something I saw today...

Something I learned today...

My favorite thing about this day...

# OUT FOR AN ADVENTURE

We are going to...

First,

Next,

Then,

Finally,

We had a great time because,

| We are going to... | We are travelling by... |
| --- | --- |
| **We are staying in...** | **We are going with...** |

# Travel Notes

Month: _____ Year: _____ Day: _____

Best thing there _____
_____
_____
_____
_____

Best food there _____
_____
_____
_____
_____

How much I spent _____
_____
_____
_____
_____

Something Learned about the place _____
_____
_____
_____
_____

Something to remember _____
_____
_____
_____
_____
_____

# ADVENTURE JOURNAL

Where we started this Morning...

Where were stopping tonight...

Something I ate today...

Something I saw today...

Something I learned today...

My favorite thing about this day...

# OUT FOR AN ADVENTURE

We are going to...

First,

Next,

Then,

Finally,

We had a great time because,

| We are going to... | We are travelling by... |
|---|---|
| **We are staying in...** | **We are going with...** |

# Travel Notes

Month:          Year:          Day:

Best thing there _____

_____

_____

_____

_____

Best food there _____

_____

_____

_____

_____

How much I spent _____

_____

_____

_____

_____

Something Learned about the place_____

_____

_____

_____

_____

Something to remember_____

_____

_____

_____

_____

_____

# ADVENTURE JOURNAL

Where we started this Morning...

Where were stopping tonight...

Something I ate today...

Something I saw today...

Something I learned today...

My favorite thing about this day...

# OUT FOR AN ADVENTURE

We are going to...

First,

Next,

Then,

Finally,

We had a great time because,

## We are going to...

## We are travelling by...

## We are staying in...

## We are going with...

# Travel Notes

Month:                Year:                Day:

Best thing there _____
_____
_____
_____
_____

Best food there _____
_____
_____
_____
_____

How much I spent _____
_____
_____
_____
_____

Something Learned about the place_____
_____
_____
_____
_____

Something to remember_____
_____
_____
_____
_____
_____

# ADVENTURE JOURNAL

Where we started this Morning...

Where were stopping tonight...

Something I ate today...

Something I saw today...

Something I learned today...

My favorite thing about this day...

# OUT FOR AN ADVENTURE

We are going to...

First,

Next,

Then,

Finally,

We had a great time because,

| We are going to... | We are travelling by... |
|---|---|
| We are staying in... | We are going with... |

# Travel Notes

Month:                    Year:                    Day:

Best thing there _____

_____
_____
_____
_____

Best food there  _____

_____
_____
_____
_____

How much I spent _____

_____
_____
_____
_____

Something Learned about the place_____

_____
_____
_____
_____

Something to remember_____

_____
_____
_____
_____
_____

# ADVENTURE JOURNAL

Where we started this Morning...

Where were stopping tonight...

Something I ate today...

Something I saw today...

Something I learned today...

My favorite thing about this day...

# OUT FOR AN ADVENTURE

We are going to...

First,

Next,

Then,

Finally,

We had a great time because,

| We are going to... | We are travelling by... |
|---|---|
| **We are staying in...** | **We are going with...** |

# Travel Notes

Month:                Year:                Day:

Best thing there _____

_____

_____

_____

_____

Best food there _____

_____

_____

_____

_____

How much I spent _____

_____

_____

_____

_____

Something Learned about the place_____

_____

_____

_____

_____

Something to remember_____

_____

_____

_____

_____

_____

# ADVENTURE JOURNAL

Where we started this Morning...

Where were stopping tonight...

Something I ate today...

Something I saw today...

Something I learned today...

My favorite thing about this day...

# OUT FOR AN ADVENTURE

We are going to...

First,

Next,

Then,

Finally,

We had a great time because,

## We are going to...

## We are travelling by...

## We are staying in...

## We are going with...

# Travel Notes

Month:                Year:                Day:

Best thing there _____

_____
_____
_____
_____

Best food there  _____

_____
_____
_____
_____

How much I spent _____

_____
_____
_____
_____

Something Learned about the place _____

_____
_____
_____
_____

Something to remember _____

_____
_____
_____
_____
_____

# ADVENTURE JOURNAL

Where we started this Morning...

Where were stopping tonight...

Something I ate today...

Something I saw today...

Something I learned today...

My favorite thing about this day...

# OUT FOR AN ADVENTURE

We are going to...

First,

Next,

Then,

Finally,

We had a great time because,

| We are going to... | We are travelling by... |
| --- | --- |
| | |

| We are  staying in... | We are going with... |
| --- | --- |
| | |

# Travel Notes

Month:                Year:                Day:

Best thing there _____

_____

_____

_____

Best food there _____

_____

_____

_____

How much I spent _____

_____

_____

_____

Something Learned about the place_____

_____

_____

_____

Something to remember _____

_____

_____

_____

_____

# ADVENTURE JOURNAL

Where we started this Morning...

Where were stopping tonight...

Something I ate today...

Something I saw today...

Something I learned today...

My favorite thing about this day...

# OUT FOR AN ADVENTURE

We are going to...

First,

Next,

Then,

Finally,

We had a great time because,

We are going to...

We are travelling by...

We are staying in...

We are going with...

# Travel Notes

Month:                Year:                Day:

Best thing there _____
_____
_____
_____
_____

Best food there  _____
_____
_____
_____
_____

How much I spent _____
_____
_____
_____
_____

Something Learned about the place_____
_____
_____
_____
_____

Something to remember_____
_____
_____
_____
_____
_____

# ADVENTURE JOURNAL

### Where we started this Morning...

### Where were stopping tonight...

### Something I ate today...

### Something I saw today...

### Something I learned today...

### My favorite thing about this day...

# OUT FOR AN ADVENTURE

We are going to...

First,

Next,

Then,

Finally,

We had a great time because,

| We are going to... | We are travelling by... |
| --- | --- |
| **We are staying in...** | **We are going with...** |

# Travel Notes

Month:                Year:                Day:

Best thing there _____
_____
_____
_____
_____

Best food there _____
_____
_____
_____
_____

How much I spent _____
_____
_____
_____
_____

Something Learned about the place_____
_____
_____
_____
_____

Something to remember_____
_____
_____
_____
_____
_____

# ADVENTURE JOURNAL

## Where we started this Morning...

## Where were stopping tonight...

## Something I ate today...

## Something I saw today...

## Something I learned today...

## My favorite thing about this day...

# OUT FOR AN ADVENTURE

We are going to...

First,

Next,

Then,

Finally,

We had a great time because,

We are going to...

We are travelling by...

We are staying in...

We are going with...

# Travel Notes

Month:                Year:                Day:

Best thing there _____

_____

_____

_____

_____

Best food there _____

_____

_____

_____

_____

How much I spent _____

_____

_____

_____

_____

Something Learned about the place_____

_____

_____

_____

_____

Something to remember _____

_____

_____

_____

_____

# ADVENTURE JOURNAL

Where we started this Morning...

Where were stopping tonight...

Something I ate today...

Something I saw today...

Something I learned today...

My favorite thing about this day...

# OUT FOR AN ADVENTURE

We are going to...

First,

Next,

Then,

Finally,

We had a great time because,

We are going to...

We are travelling by...

We are staying in...

We are going with...

# Travel Notes

Month:                Year:                Day:

Best thing there _____
_____
_____
_____
_____

Best food there  _____
_____
_____
_____
_____

How much I spent _____
_____
_____
_____
_____

Something Learned about the place_____
_____
_____
_____
_____

Something to remember_____
_____
_____
_____
_____
_____

# ADVENTURE JOURNAL

Where we started this Morning...

Where were stopping tonight...

Something I ate today...

Something I saw today...

Something I learned today...

My favorite thing about this day...

# OUT FOR AN ADVENTURE

We are going to...

First,

Next,

Then,

Finally,

We had a great time because,

We are going to...

We are travelling by...

We are staying in...

We are going with...

# Travel Notes

Month:                Year:                Day:

Best thing there _____

_____
_____
_____
_____

Best food there  _____

_____
_____
_____
_____

How much I spent _____

_____
_____
_____
_____

Something Learned about the place_____

_____
_____
_____
_____

Something to remember_____

_____
_____
_____
_____
_____

# ADVENTURE JOURNAL

Where we started this Morning...

Where were stopping tonight...

Something I ate today...

Something I saw today...

Something I learned today...

My favorite thing about this day...

# OUT FOR AN ADVENTURE

We are going to...

First,

Next,

Then,

Finally,

We had a great time because,

## We are going to...

## We are travelling by...

## We are staying in...

## We are going with...

# Travel Notes

Month:                Year:                Day:

Best thing there _____
_____
_____
_____
_____

Best food there  _____
_____
_____
_____
_____

How much I spent _____
_____
_____
_____
_____

Something Learned about the place_____
_____
_____
_____
_____

Something to remember_____
_____
_____
_____
_____
_____

# ADVENTURE JOURNAL

| Where we started this Morning... | Where were stopping tonight... |
|---|---|
| | |

| Something I ate today... | Something I saw today... |
|---|---|
| | |

| Something I learned today... | My favorite thing about this day... |
|---|---|
| | |

# OUT FOR AN ADVENTURE

We are going to...

First,

Next,

Then,

Finally,

We had a great time because,

We are going to...

We are travelling by...

We are staying in...

We are going with...

# Travel Notes

Month:                  Year:                          Day:

Best thing there _____

_____

_____

_____

_____

Best food there  _____

_____

_____

_____

_____

How much I spent _____

_____

_____

_____

_____

Something Learned about the place_____

_____

_____

_____

_____

Something to remember_____

_____

_____

_____

_____

_____

# ADVENTURE JOURNAL

Where we started this Morning...

Where were stopping tonight...

Something I ate today...

Something I saw today...

Something I learned today...

My favorite thing about this day...

# OUT FOR AN ADVENTURE

We are going to...

First,

Next,

Then,

Finally,

We had a great time because,

| We are going to... | We are travelling by... |
| --- | --- |
| We are staying in... | We are going with... |

# Travel Notes

Month:                Year:                Day:

Best thing there _____
_____
_____
_____

Best food there  _____
_____
_____
_____

How much I spent _____
_____
_____
_____

Something Learned about the place_____
_____
_____
_____

Something to remember _____
_____
_____
_____
_____

# ADVENTURE JOURNAL

Where we started this Morning...

Where were stopping tonight...

Something I ate today...

Something I saw today...

Something I learned today...

My favorite thing about this day...

# OUT FOR AN ADVENTURE

We are going to...

First,

Next,

Then,

Finally,

We had a great time because,

| We are going to... | We are travelling by... |
|---|---|
| We are staying in... | We are going with... |

# Travel Notes

Month:            Year:            Day:

Best thing there _____

_____

_____

_____

Best food there _____

_____

_____

_____

How much I spent _____

_____

_____

_____

Something Learned about the place_____

_____

_____

_____

Something to remember_____

_____

_____

_____

_____

# ADVENTURE JOURNAL

Where we started this Morning...

Where were stopping tonight...

Something I ate today...

Something I saw today...

Something I learned today...

My favorite thing about this day...

# OUT FOR AN ADVENTURE

We are going to...

First,

Next,

Then,

Finally,

We had a great time because,

We are going to...

We are travelling by...

We are staying in...

We are going with...

# Travel Notes

Month:        Year:        Day:

Best thing there _____

_____

_____

_____

_____

Best food there _____

_____

_____

_____

_____

How much I spent _____

_____

_____

_____

_____

Something Learned about the place_____

_____

_____

_____

_____

Something to remember_____

_____

_____

_____

_____

_____

# ADVENTURE JOURNAL

Where we started this Morning...

Where were stopping tonight...

Something I ate today...

Something I saw today...

Something I learned today...

My favorite thing about this day...

# OUT FOR AN ADVENTURE

We are going to...

First,

Next,

Then,

Finally,

We had a great time because,

| We are going to... | We are travelling by... |
|---|---|
| | |

| We are  staying in... | We are going with... |
|---|---|
| | |

# Travel Notes

Month:          Year:          Day:

Best thing there _____

_____

_____

_____

Best food there _____

_____

_____

_____

How much I spent _____

_____

_____

_____

Something Learned about the place_____

_____

_____

_____

Something to remember_____

_____

_____

_____

_____

# ADVENTURE JOURNAL

Where we started this Morning...

Where were stopping tonight...

Something I ate today...

Something I saw today...

Something I learned today...

My favorite thing about this day...

# OUT FOR AN ADVENTURE

We are going to...

First,

Next,

Then,

Finally,

We had a great time because,

| We are going to... | We are travelling by... |
|---|---|
| We are staying in... | We are going with... |

# Travel Notes

Month: _____ Year: _____ Day: _____

Best thing there _____
_____
_____
_____
_____

Best food there _____
_____
_____
_____
_____

How much I spent _____
_____
_____
_____
_____

Something Learned about the place_____
_____
_____
_____
_____

Something to remember_____
_____
_____
_____
_____
_____

# ADVENTURE JOURNAL

Where we started this Morning...

Where were stopping tonight...

Something I ate today...

Something I saw today...

Something I learned today...

My favorite thing about this day...

# OUT FOR AN ADVENTURE

We are going to...

First,

Next,

Then,

Finally,

We had a great time because,

| We are going to... | We are travelling by... |
| We are  staying in... | We are going with... |

# Travel Notes

Month: _____ Year: _____ Day: _____

Best thing there _____

_____

_____

_____

_____

Best food there _____

_____

_____

_____

_____

How much I spent _____

_____

_____

_____

_____

Something Learned about the place_____

_____

_____

_____

_____

Something to remember_____

_____

_____

_____

_____

_____

# ADVENTURE JOURNAL

Where we started this Morning...

Where were stopping tonight...

Something I ate today...

Something I saw today...

Something I learned today...

My favorite thing about this day...

# OUT FOR AN ADVENTURE

We are going to...

First,

Next,

Then,

Finally,

We had a great time because,

| We are going to... | We are travelling by... |
|---|---|
| **We are staying in...** | **We are going with...** |

# Travel Notes

Month:                Year:                Day:

Best thing there _____
_____
_____
_____
_____

Best food there _____
_____
_____
_____
_____

How much I spent _____
_____
_____
_____
_____

Something Learned about the place_____
_____
_____
_____
_____

Something to remember_____
_____
_____
_____
_____
_____

# ADVENTURE JOURNAL

Where we started this Morning...

Where were stopping tonight...

Something I ate today...

Something I saw today...

Something I learned today...

My favorite thing about this day...

# OUT FOR AN ADVENTURE

We are going to...

First,

Next,

Then,

Finally,

We had a great time because,

We are going to...

We are travelling by...

We are  staying in...

We are going with...

# Travel Notes

Month: _____ Year: _____ Day: _____

Best thing there _____

_____

_____

_____

_____

Best food there _____

_____

_____

_____

_____

How much I spent _____

_____

_____

_____

_____

Something Learned about the place_____

_____

_____

_____

Something to remember_____

_____

_____

_____

_____

_____

# ADVENTURE JOURNAL

Where we started this Morning...

Where were stopping tonight...

Something I ate today...

Something I saw today...

Something I learned today...

My favorite thing about this day...

# OUT FOR AN ADVENTURE

We are going to...

First,

Next,

Then,

Finally,

We had a great time because,

| We are going to... | We are travelling by... |
|---|---|
| We are staying in... | We are going with... |

# Travel Notes

Month:                    Year:                    Day:

Best thing there _____
_____
_____
_____
_____

Best food there _____
_____
_____
_____
_____

How much I spent _____
_____
_____
_____
_____

Something Learned about the place_____
_____
_____
_____
_____

Something to remember_____
_____
_____
_____
_____
_____

# ADVENTURE JOURNAL

Where we started this Morning...

Where were stopping tonight...

Something I ate today...

Something I saw today...

Something I learned today...

My favorite thing about this day...

# OUT FOR AN ADVENTURE

We are going to...

First,

Next,

Then,

Finally,

We had a great time because,

We are going to...

We are travelling by...

We are staying in...

We are going with...

# Travel Notes

Month:                    Year:                    Day:

Best thing there _____
_____
_____
_____
_____

Best food there _____
_____
_____
_____
_____

How much I spent _____
_____
_____
_____
_____

Something Learned about the place_____
_____
_____
_____
_____

Something to remember _____
_____
_____
_____
_____
_____

# ADVENTURE JOURNAL

Where we started this Morning...

Where were stopping tonight...

Something I ate today...

Something I saw today...

Something I learned today...

My favorite thing about this day...

# OUT FOR AN ADVENTURE

We are going to...

First,

Next,

Then,

Finally,

We had a great time because,

## We are going to...

## We are travelling by...

## We are staying in...

## We are going with...

# Travel Notes

Month:       Year:       Day:

Best thing there _____

_____

_____

_____

_____

Best food there _____

_____

_____

_____

_____

How much I spent _____

_____

_____

_____

_____

Something Learned about the place_____

_____

_____

_____

_____

Something to remember_____

_____

_____

_____

_____

_____

# ADVENTURE JOURNAL

Where we started this Morning...

Where were stopping tonight...

Something I ate today...

Something I saw today...

Something I learned today...

My favorite thing about this day...

# OUT FOR AN ADVENTURE

We are going to...

First,

Next,

Then,

Finally,

We had a great time because,

| We are going to... | We are travelling by... |
|---|---|
| | |

| We are staying in... | We are going with... |
|---|---|
| | |

# Travel Notes

Month:                Year:                Day:

Best thing there _____
_____
_____
_____
_____

Best food there _____
_____
_____
_____
_____

How much I spent _____
_____
_____
_____
_____

Something Learned about the place_____
_____
_____
_____
_____

Something to remember _____
_____
_____
_____
_____
_____

# ADVENTURE JOURNAL

Where we started this Morning...

Where were stopping tonight...

Something I ate today...

Something I saw today...

Something I learned today...

My favorite thing about this day...

# OUT FOR AN ADVENTURE

We are going to...

First,

Next,

Then,

Finally,

We had a great time because,

| We are going to... | We are travelling by... |
| We are staying in... | We are going with... |

# Travel Notes

Month:                Year:                Day:

Best thing there _____
_____
_____
_____
_____

Best food there _____
_____
_____
_____
_____

How much I spent _____
_____
_____
_____
_____

Something Learned about the place_____
_____
_____
_____
_____

Something to remember_____
_____
_____
_____
_____
_____

# ADVENTURE JOURNAL

Where we started this Morning...

Where were stopping tonight...

Something I ate today...

Something I saw today...

Something I learned today...

My favorite thing about this day...

# OUT FOR AN ADVENTURE

We are going to...

First,

Next,

Then,

Finally,

We had a great time because,

## We are going to...

## We are travelling by...

## We are staying in...

## We are going with...

CPSIA information can be obtained
at www.ICGtesting.com
Printed in the USA
LVHW020102290822
726977LV00009B/560